One Jump Ahead

One Jump Ahead

WHAT IT TAKES TO BE A SHOWJUMPER

Jean Germany

Illustrated with photographs by Mayotte Magnus

A Children's Book from
W. H. ALLEN & Co. Ltd
A Howard & Wyndham Company
1979

Text of book copyright © 1979 by Jean Germany

Photographs copyright © 1979 by Mayotte Magnus

Photographs on pp 66 & 67 copyright © Findlay Davidson
Photographs on p 38 copyright © Syndication International

Designed by Logos Design, Datchet

This book or parts thereof may not be reproduced in
any form whatsoever without permission in writing

Typeset by Computacomp (UK) Ltd,
Fort William, Scotland
Printed in Great Britain by
Caledonian Graphics Ltd

for the publishers, W. H. Allen & Co. Ltd,
44 Hill Street, London W1X 8LB

Bound by
Hunter & Fowlis, Edinburgh

ISBN 0 491 02147 X

p 69, bottom picture, Leslie Lane, the official Wembley photographer
p 89, far right, Eddie Macken

Contents

1	Life at Home	6
2	Relaxing with the Family	18
3	Training at Home and at Stoneleigh	26
4	Horses	38
5	Preparing for Show	42
6	National Events	50
7	International Events	58
8	Wembley – Outside the Ring with the Personalities	68
9	Wembley – Competing	80

1·Life at Home

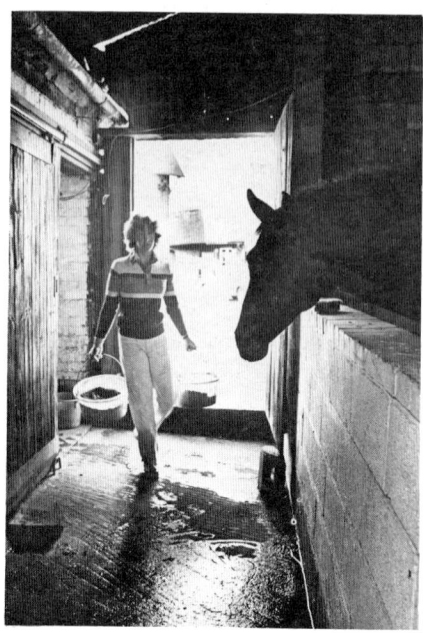

I am eighteen years old, and a competitive showjumper. When I was ten, jumping with my very first pony, I thought that there was nothing more exciting in the world than being a showjumper. But the past eight years have taught me that showjumping is a lot of hard work – for every moment of jumping and winning, there are thousands of minutes of preparation and training. It seems that you are only a champion for seconds; all too soon you are very firmly back to earth, brushing, cleaning and feeding. Still, for me, the horses make all the hard work worthwhile, and I like my life.

This book will show you exactly the kind of life I lead as a young showjumper.

Take my typical day at home in Nottinghamshire...

I begin each and every morning feeding and watering the horses, and mucking out their boxes. We keep five on the farm, and this year I have mainly jumped with three. The others are too young and untrained. Occasionally one becomes too old, and we use him just for hunting. My family is not rich, and we can only afford to keep so many horses because people interested in showjumping buy them for me. I then train and jump the horses for them.

The horses' feed often varies, but usually it is a mixture of oats, bran, sugar-beet pulp and nuts, plus cod liver oil and salt when necessary. They are fed three times a day. If Jill and I are away, my mother or my father do it for me. I have two brothers, but their interest in horses is limited to riding for fun and hunting. One of the most interesting things about horses is that they all have such distinct personalities. For example, some gobble their food quickly, others prefer to take their time, and one horse I had wouldn't eat until my back was turned – I could never watch him. So, depending on the horses' eating habits, I find I sometimes have to leave the buckets in the stalls all day.

Next, I fill the hay nets and hang one in each stall for the horse to nibble at throughout the day. Again, we are lucky to have a farm – hay and straw can be a big expense in keeping a horse.

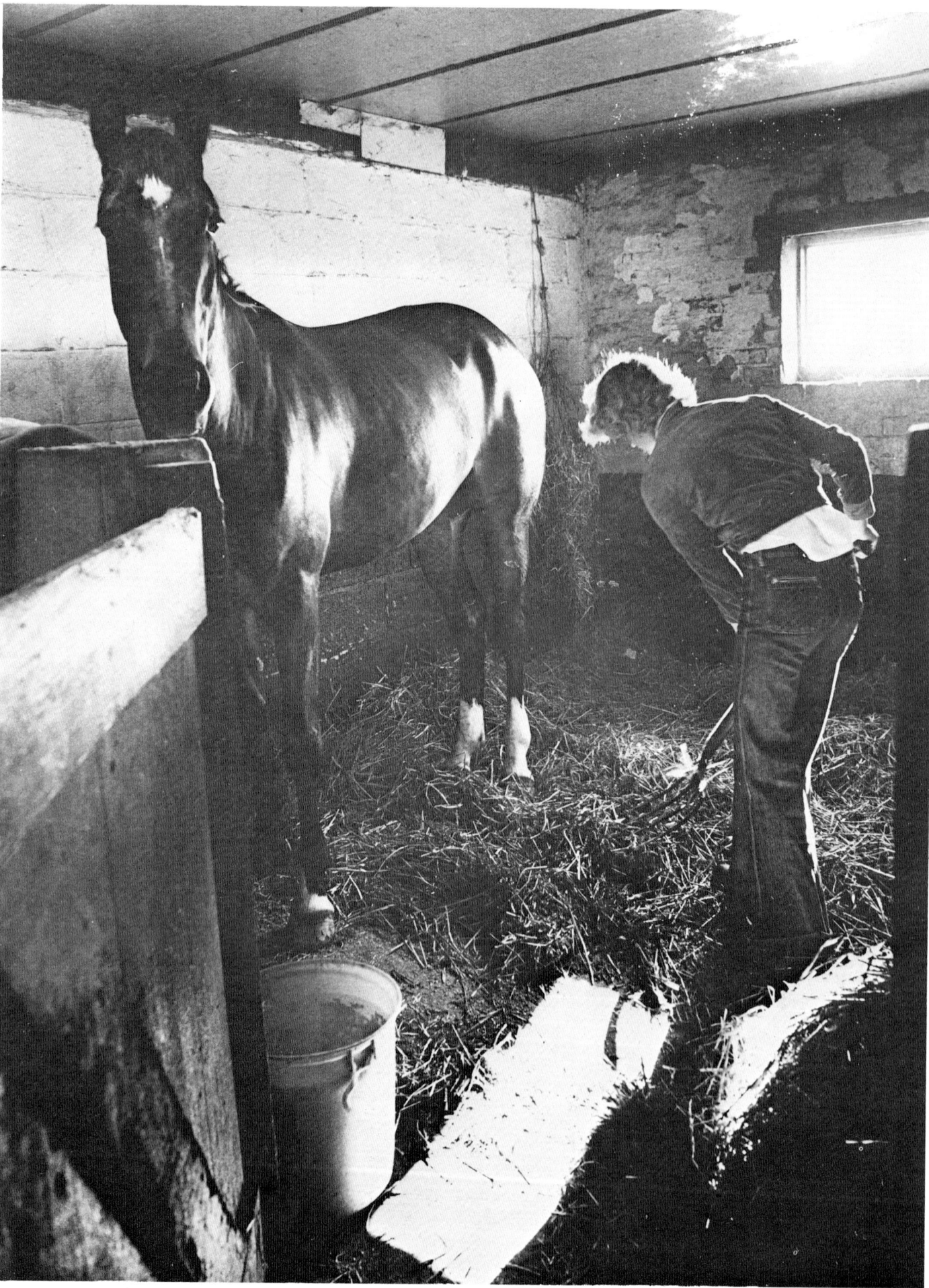

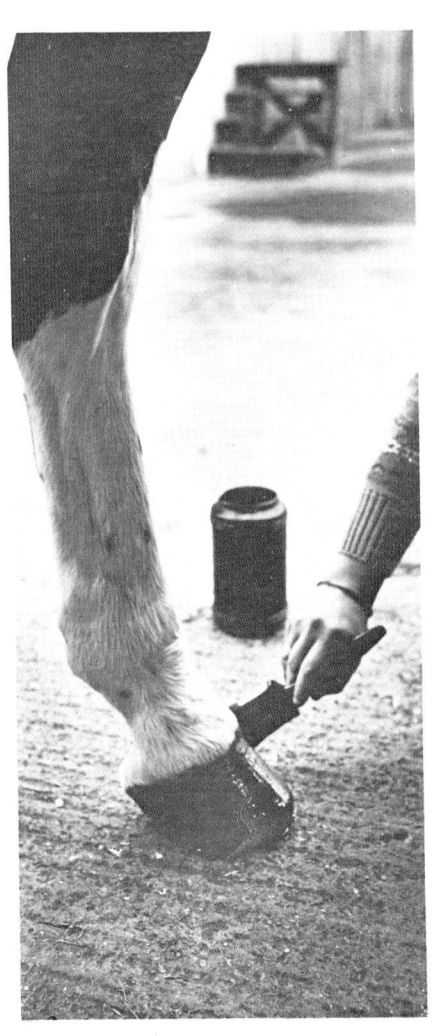

Mucking out is one of the things everyone seems to hate doing. It is a bit messy and smelly, I'll admit, but I don't really mind doing it for the horses. Jill and I do it thoroughly once a day. This means shovelling all the dirty straw into a barrow, which we take out into the yard and empty on to the muck heap. We then replace this with nice clean straw. In the evening we just turn the straw over and take the droppings out. It is very important to keep the horses' stables clean, otherwise standing in dirty wet straw for hours on end can give them thrush (foot rot). The horse in the picture is Sabbath. He's a lovely gentle thing and one of those horses who loves to jump. As soon as he's in the ring, he can hardly wait to begin.

We also pick out the horses' feet every day, removing stones and bits of grit which if not attended to can cause lameness. The hooves are also oiled every day to prevent their cracking and getting brittle. This stimulates growth and keeps them looking smart. Once every six weeks the hooves are filed, as they grow much like fingernails. The farrier, who looks after the horses' feet, usually does this every time the horse goes to be shod.

If mucking out is the one thing everyone hates, brushing is the one thing everyone loves. It's lovely to see the change it makes in the horse's coat. When you brush you are actually cleaning the horse, and his coat can turn from being dull and lifeless to glossy and sleek, in a matter of minutes.

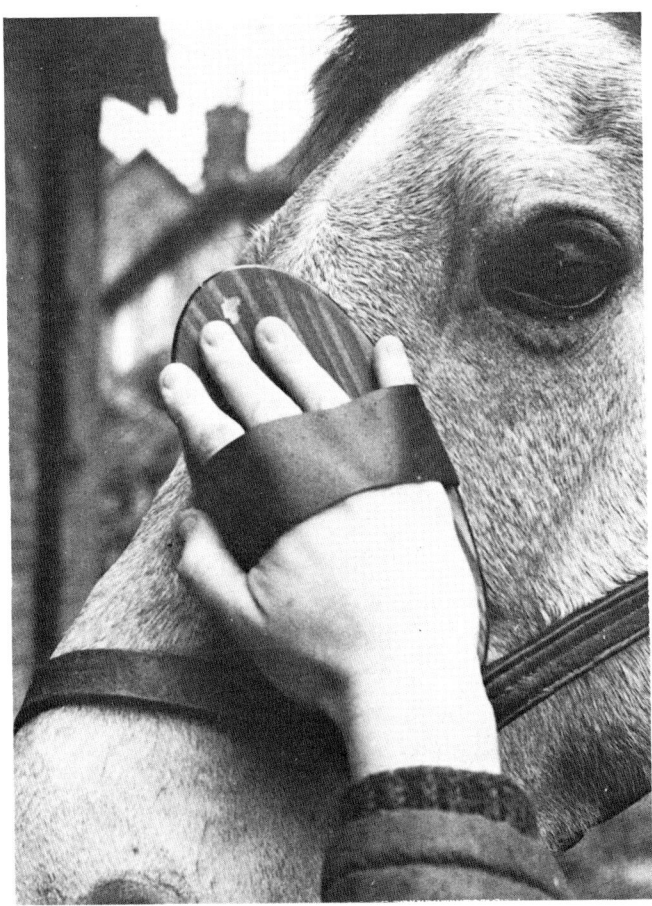

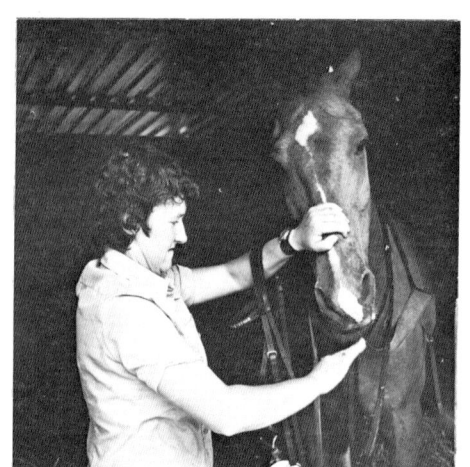

After we do all the morning chores and have a cup of tea or coffee, and perhaps exercise the horses, it is time for their second feed. Usually by this time in the day I'm not so rushed, so the horses and I have longer chats. This may sound silly, but they love to be talked to and I think it's very important as it helps to build up a strong relationship between yourself and the horse, which is vital when you are in the ring jumping with them.

Often Jill and I put vaseline around the horse's mouth. In the summer when we are doing a lot of shows, the bit can create sores, and the vaseline helps protect and heal their mouths. Jill has lived with our family for seven years and, besides being part of the family, she is invaluable with the horses.

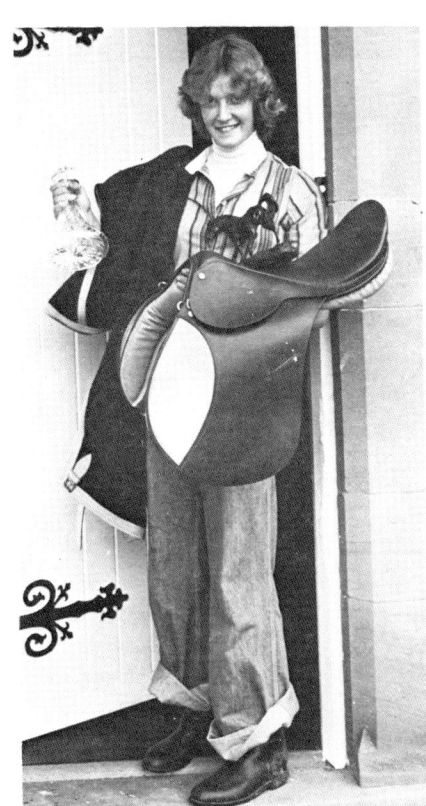

Cleaning the tack should be done regularly, and is really an essential part of the routine of looking after a horse. First it is washed, then saddle soap is used – the leather always feels so much softer and smoother after using the saddle soap and rubbing it dry. Then finally I polish the bits and the stirrups.

During the main show season we try to do all the tack every day. Jason, the dog, is my constant companion. He loves to follow me everywhere. My family always says, when you see Jason, you see Jean. Dogs and horses seem to go together. Even on the circuit everyone seems to bring their dog or dogs!

The last picture at the left is really just for the photographer. It is a collection of some of the loot I've won this year from the European Championships. Basically, I enter as many shows as possible in the hope of winning enough prize money to qualify for the more important shows. My mum and dad and I work out which are the best shows to go in for. Of course, you have to be invited to a number of the bigger shows. I've been lucky for the past several years and have done well enough to be invited to most of the important ones.

We think our vet, Jim Patterson, is the best in the country. This particular day, one of the horses had gone lame, so Jim came and removed its shoe and gave it a complete check-up. Jim has a nice easy manner with the horses. His jokes make me laugh, and the horses obviously feel at ease with him.

The horse has a very delicate anatomy, and if anything seems the slightest bit wrong, we always ring for Jim. For showjumping the horses must be in peak physical condition.

Checking the horse's mouth gives a good indication of his health. If something is wrong internally, it usually shows up in the condition of the teeth, gums, tongue or throat.

I've had several ponies and horses which had not been given proper care. One was over-ridden, and one was just a little neglected. Usually, it takes a long time to correct and train a horse with a poor background. There is no way of knowing what a horse is going to be like until you have had it for some time. You can't check all the details of its history, and some people do forget important facts when they advertise the sale of a horse, although you can be certain that the more expensive it is, the better its pedigree is. Then, different horses respond to different riders. So, to a certain extent, getting a first-class horse is a matter of luck. There are a number of young riders who are very good, but it is the horse that finally makes the difference between winning and losing.

You may have noticed that most of the horses I've mentioned have been male. This is because mares tend to be either/or — either very good, or very temperamental and difficult. I've always had more luck with the geldings, and at present that is all we keep.

The next page is a series of shots with me and Sabbath. In one photograph I'm also bringing in the straw for the bedding, and later taking a break to reflect on the next show with the horses.

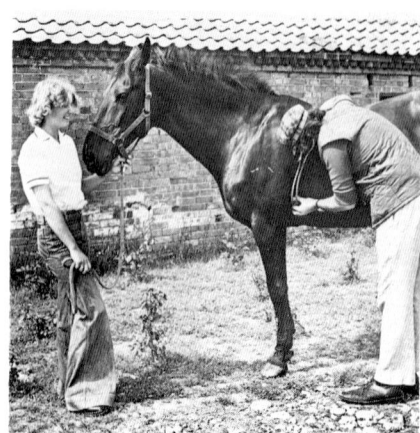

Horses are always curious and always alert to what's going on. Sometimes I think they are a bit jealous when one horse is getting more attention than they are. Here, I'm preparing to exercise Magie, and Sabbath is looking distinctly wistful!

Besides providing hay and straw, a farm gives me the advantage of being able to exercise the horses either in nearby woods or on the land itself. When we're home, this is my favourite activity (despite the flies I'm flicking off Sabbath). A very special bond grows between you and the horse in the quiet of the countryside, where you can both enjoy the sky, the trees, and the summer sounds away from the hurly-burly of competitive riding.

Such exercise is also vital to the conditioning of the horse. It's a refreshing activity after the long road trips where he has to stand in a stuffy horse box, and a good break from the boring stables and training routine when we are actually at the shows.

Since the whole family rides, with Jill included, we can always give the horses a good exercise every day.

2·Relaxing with the Family

MY MUM, DAD, JILL AND I are on the road so much of the year that having a meal at home with all of the family is a treat. Here, my twin brother, John, my younger brother, Chris, and a family friend enjoy the Sunday lunch. My mother is a very good cook, and it makes such a pleasant change from all the quick snack meals we snatch at the shows. Although we cook in our caravan when we're on the road, Mum is obviously too busy to cook as she does at home, and anyway, she hasn't got the proper facilities.

My brother John used to jump ponies with me when we were both ten. Then he lost interest in competitive riding and two years later he gave it up, just at the time the showjumping bug really got into my blood. I started to live for all the shows; I loved anything to do with ponies and horses.

Looking back now, I think I've been extremely fortunate. My parents have always supported, helped and encouraged me with all my showjumping activities. Each year it has become more and more time-consuming, and Dad has gradually re-scheduled more and more of the farm work to enable him to accompany me on the dozens of trips we take. The trips mean a heavier work load for Mum as well. She has to run the house and all that goes with it, as well as all the extra work involved with our travels in the caravan, and the growing demands of showjumping administration.

The first two years I became active in showjumping and pony club events, I tried to keep up with all my school work. I would miss a few days here and there, and I'd always try and catch up with anything I'd missed. However, after a bit it became hopeless, and eventually I had to have a private tutor to study for my 'O' levels. Again, I'm grateful to my parents – they knew I was more interested in showjumping than in continuing my studies. Other parents might have insisted that I stayed at school and forgot about showjumping altogether.

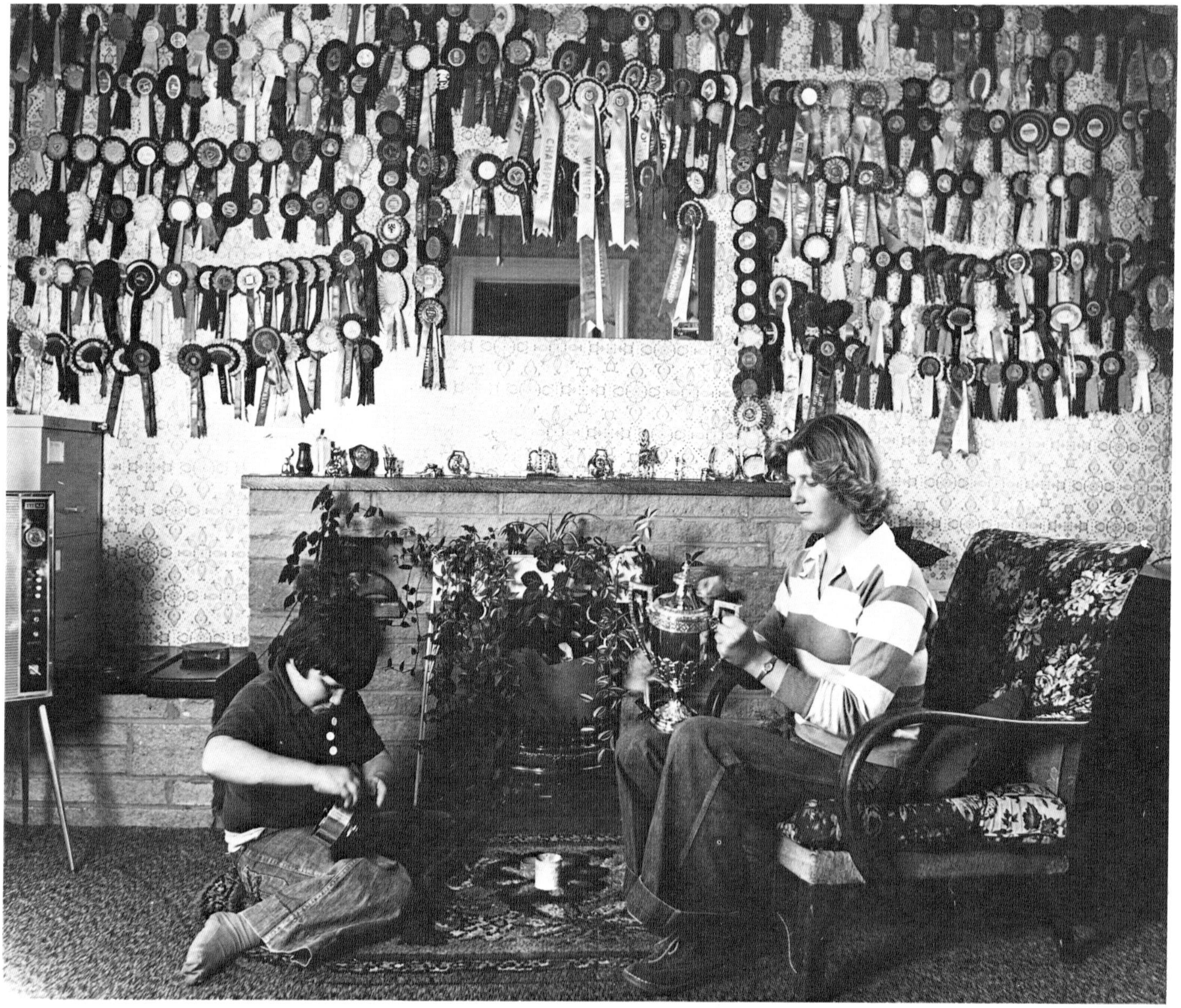

Behind me you can see some of my rosettes, and the various awards on the mantelpiece. Sometimes it rather takes my breath away to think I've won all this! When I look closely I can usually remember the event, and the horse I was riding. Chris sometimes helps me polish the trophies. After cleaning the tack and grooming the horses, this isn't a task I really like, but Mum insists, and it is nice to see all the cups gleaming!

So far, Chris hasn't shown any interest in ponies or horses. He's too busy growing up and struggling with his Latin verbs.

Occasionally, John challenges me to a game of snooker. He usually wins, though I'm not all that bad. John is an apprentice mechanic and, like the rest of us, his favourite relaxation is flopping in front of the television.

When it comes to reading, I usually choose something about horses. I used to read a lot of pony stories, but now I mainly like factual books. I have come to like reading travel books, too. I first went to Europe four years ago with the British Junior Team, and I love visiting some of the historical sites if I can find the time.

Often, after all the travelling and the shows, I find myself fast asleep in a chair in front of the television. Our routine can be most exhausting!

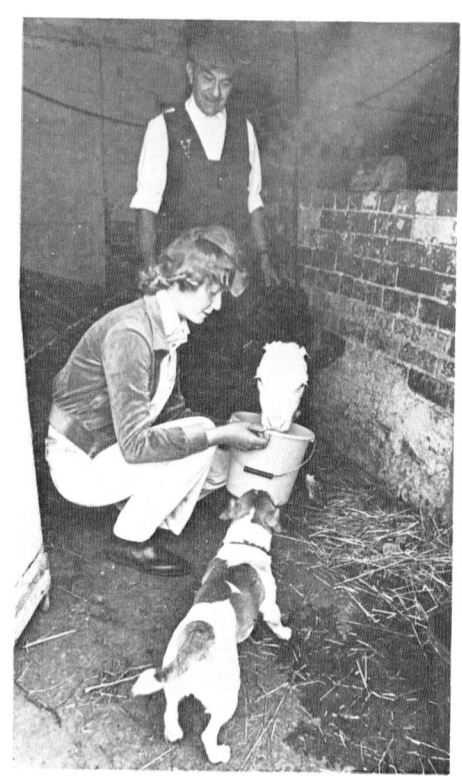

When we are at home, the whole family likes to help with the farm work whenever possible. Chris and I and one of our neighbours, Mr Brown, are helping to get in the harvest. Not that we don't have a few moments to spare for sheer high spirits – one of the best things about farming is the exhilarating feeling you get from the smells, the fresh air and the countryside. All of my family feel a certain amount of pride in our Nottinghamshire origins and land. With all the travelling we do, and after all the excitement of the showjumping circuit, there is nothing like coming home.

When I'm home I often go to my grandparents' farm for a visit. They are only a short distance away – just right for a gentle canter on horseback. Even though we have calves of our own, I love helping Grandpa feed his.

One of our biggest chores after a show is the endless laundry involved. Since every time you jump you must appear spotless, and since you may be showing several horses multiplied by several events, the number of times you change your outfit on a rainy day doesn't bear thinking about!

Jill and I manage to cover quite a bit of countryside when we are exercising the horses. There is a stately home nearby and we often pass by it, but I think our very favourite place is the woods. I'm riding Sabbath, and Jill is on Janus. I have high hopes for Janus. He was bought for me by a Mr Appleyard last year, and is a New Zealand bred horse. He has only been jumping for two years, and already he shows great promise.

When Janus arrived last October, I jumped him for about a month, and then turned him out for the winter. This is another reason for keeping so many horses. They need to have a break from time to time. Depending on the circumstances, we may give a horse a couple of months off, but sometimes they need much longer. After Olympia in December, the indoor circuit of big shows is almost finished, and the outdoor circuit doesn't begin again until March. This is the slackest period of the showjumping year, and we use this to give as many of the horses as possible a break. Again, everyone in the family keeps a very close eye on the horses throughout the year so that they are jumped or rested according to their condition.

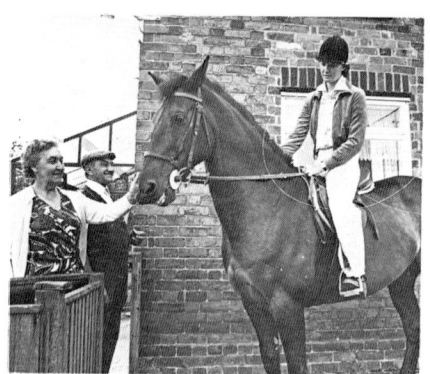

3·Training at Home and at Stoneleigh

ON TOP OF ALL THE GROOMING, cleaning and general exercise the horses are given, it is also necessary to train each horse on a regular basis. This improves their ability to understand all the various body signals I give them, keeps them supple for the shows, and helps prepare them to anticipate various kinds of jumps. Obviously, Jill and I prepare the training according to the skill and ability of each horse.

Compared with most other professions, showjumping does not give beginners a great deal of professional advice and training. Some riders may learn a fair amount at pony clubs, but most of my experience has come from just taking the pony and jumping – sort of trial and error. I had been jumping for four years before I actually had any professional instruction. The British Showjumping Association started a scheme to train young people between the ages of fourteen and sixteen. I was chosen, with five others, out of seventeen pupils to further this initial training with five weeks' coaching by Lars Sederholm. Before this course, I never knew how to half-halt. This is slowing the horse down at the pace which you are going (but not stopping) and pushing it forward again. This brings the horse on the bit. I was also given instruction on flat work (a form of exercise to keep the horse supple) and making the horse jump through grids to improve his balance. It does seem a bit incredible that there are so few courses for aspiring riders, when you think of how much coaching tennis, football, swimming or almost any other sport entails.

Jill and I use all the exercises I've been shown, and a few of our own, in the yard near the stables. In the first two pictures I'm lunging on Magie. Lunging is an exercise which is good for the rider and the horse. It strengthens the balance and muscles of the rider and improves the seat, as well as helping to keep the horse supple.

We have an area of sandy ground set aside for the school. On the following page you can see how we use this school for actual jumping practice. I'm training my novice horse, Quarter Sessions. Quarter Sessions is classed as a Grade C horse as he

has yet to win a significant amount of money at any of the shows. As soon as he wins £200, he will be graded a B horse, and as soon as he wins £400 he'll be graded an A horse. To qualify for the Royal International Horse Show every rider must go through a series of Area International Trials (AIT), and to enter any of these the horse must have an A grade. This is another good reason for having several horses, and for rotating them according to how well they are performing. Almost everyone in showjumping keeps one novice horse to train for the future, hoping that it will eventually be classed as a Grade A horse.

Twice a year, the British Showjumping Association organises several courses run by Dick Stillwell, the well-known British showjumping trainer, for promising young riders. These are four-day courses taken at the National Equestrian Centre in Stoneleigh. For these courses you send in your name to the training committee and then are selected and told if you are on the course a few weeks before you are due to go. Usually, you take a novice or a fairly inexperienced horse.

Dick Stillwell is an extremely strict trainer, sometimes reminding me of a movie director from the 1930s. He is very sharp and keeps us all on our toes. However, we all know that underneath he cares for us, and wants us to do well. I have enormous respect for him, and feel that he has taught me a great deal about showjumping.

On the first day we start by doing flat or ground work – exercises with no jumping involved, designed to improve the horse's suppleness and balance. When you sit on a horse you, as a rider, change its balance, and it is therefore necessary for the horse to develop muscles (extra ones, if you like) in its neck, back, and hind legs. When a horse is correctly exercised and its back has the correct curve, it can jump comfortably. An unschooled horse will have more muscles underneath its neck and will hold its head too high ('above the bit') or too low ('on its forehead'). You can see the correct position from the photograph – the flat of its face is vertical to the ground and its neck is arched. This is called 'on the bit'.

It is best if the horse follows a gradual training programme, which is why Jill and I continue to train at home after all the courses. The exercises include increasing and decreasing the horse's pace, circling, turning and going up and down slopes. By circling and turning to the left and to the right, the horse gradually finds it more comfortable to drop its head and accept the bit. In the photograph you can see me circling on the horse.

A horse can only be schooled for short periods and needs rest at frequent intervals. Like humans, horses get bored with routine work. Exercising across country and hunting are the best methods of continuing a horse's training. Hunting is especially helpful, as the horse follows experienced horses which helps it to overcome its fear of jumping.

Only after you have given the horse this ground or flat work is it really ready to jump. At Stoneleigh we usually start jumping the second day. First we work out over poles laid at ground level. This encourages the horse to pick up its feet and use the muscles in its back. Then we walk the horse over small jumps called cavalletti. Gradually the obstacles become more complicated with the width becoming more important than the height. This is because the horse must put more effort into clearing a spread than clearing an upright. Next comes a series of obstacles called a grid. The grid is formed so that there are only a few spaces between each obstacle, and the horse must land and immediately jump again. You can see a grid on the next page beginning the series of small photographs. Once the horse has accomplished this series of exercises, it can be faced with higher jumps.

In the small pictures on the side of this page is a series of close-ups of the different boots which protect the horse when it jumps: brushing boots, Yorkshire boots, and overreach boots (this horse also has exercise bandages on to protect its forelegs from strain).

One of the best exercises a rider can do is to go without the stirrups. This improves your own balance and agility.

To encourage a horse frightened to jump over water, the horse is made to walk in a small area in front of the jump. This area is enclosed by people and poles. The horse is thus forced to take the jump and gradually it will gain confidence to go over the jump on its own.

In the large photograph you can see how the horse is taking the jump with the correct bend in his back. Also note the approach pole which helps the horse prepare for the jump.

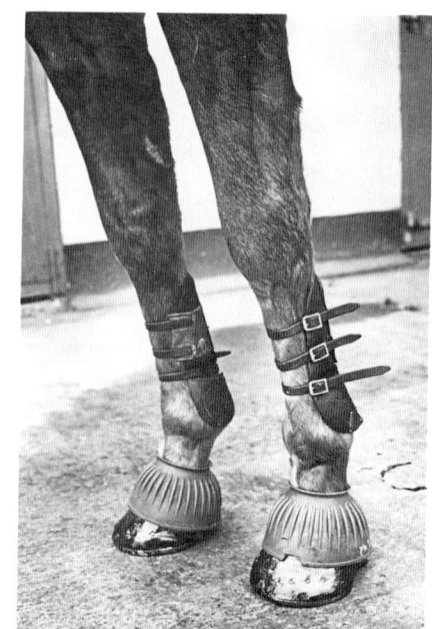

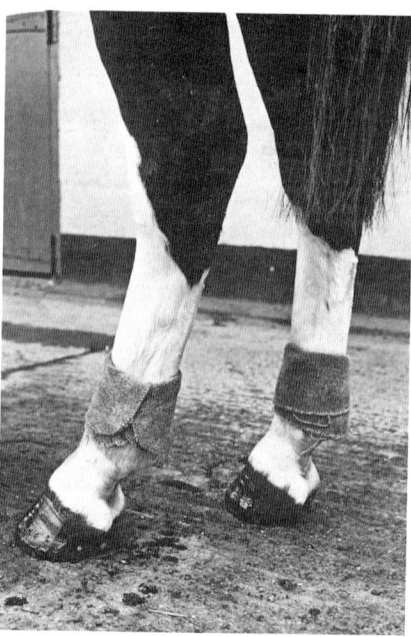

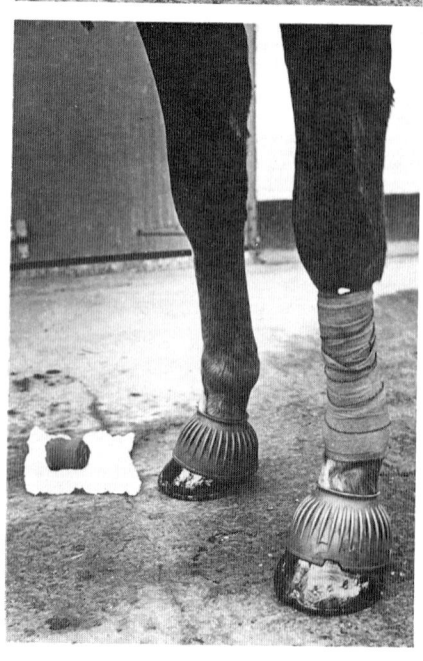

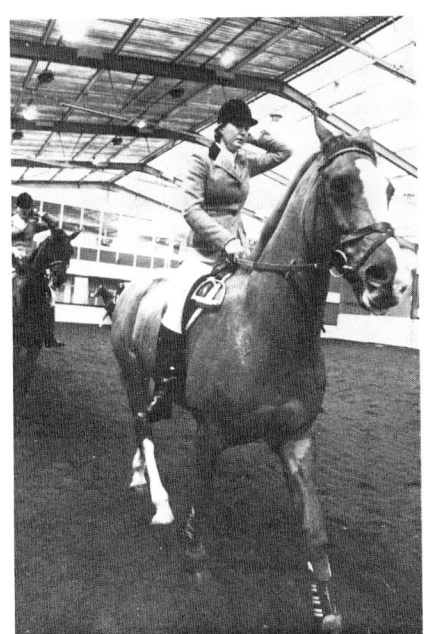

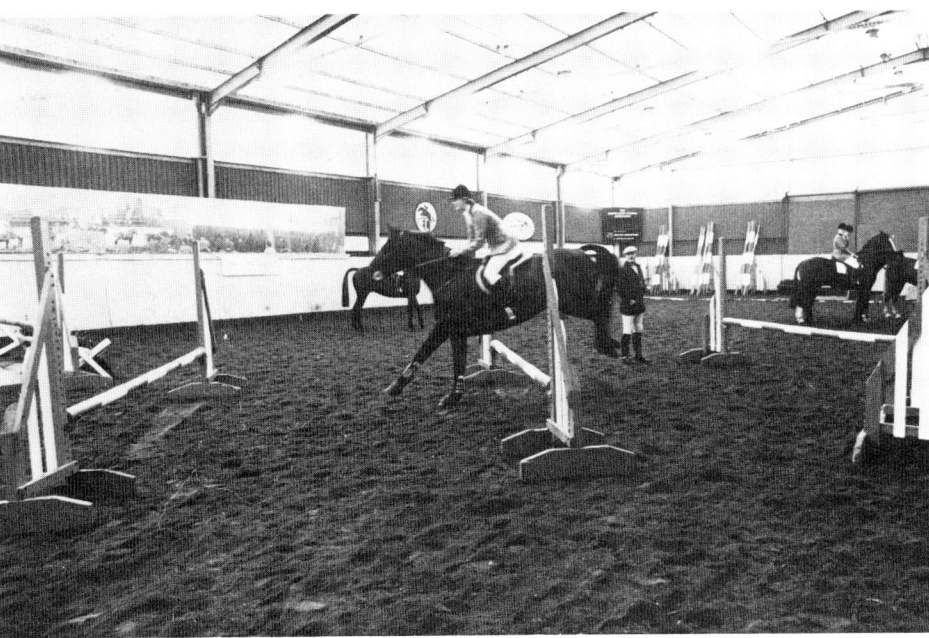

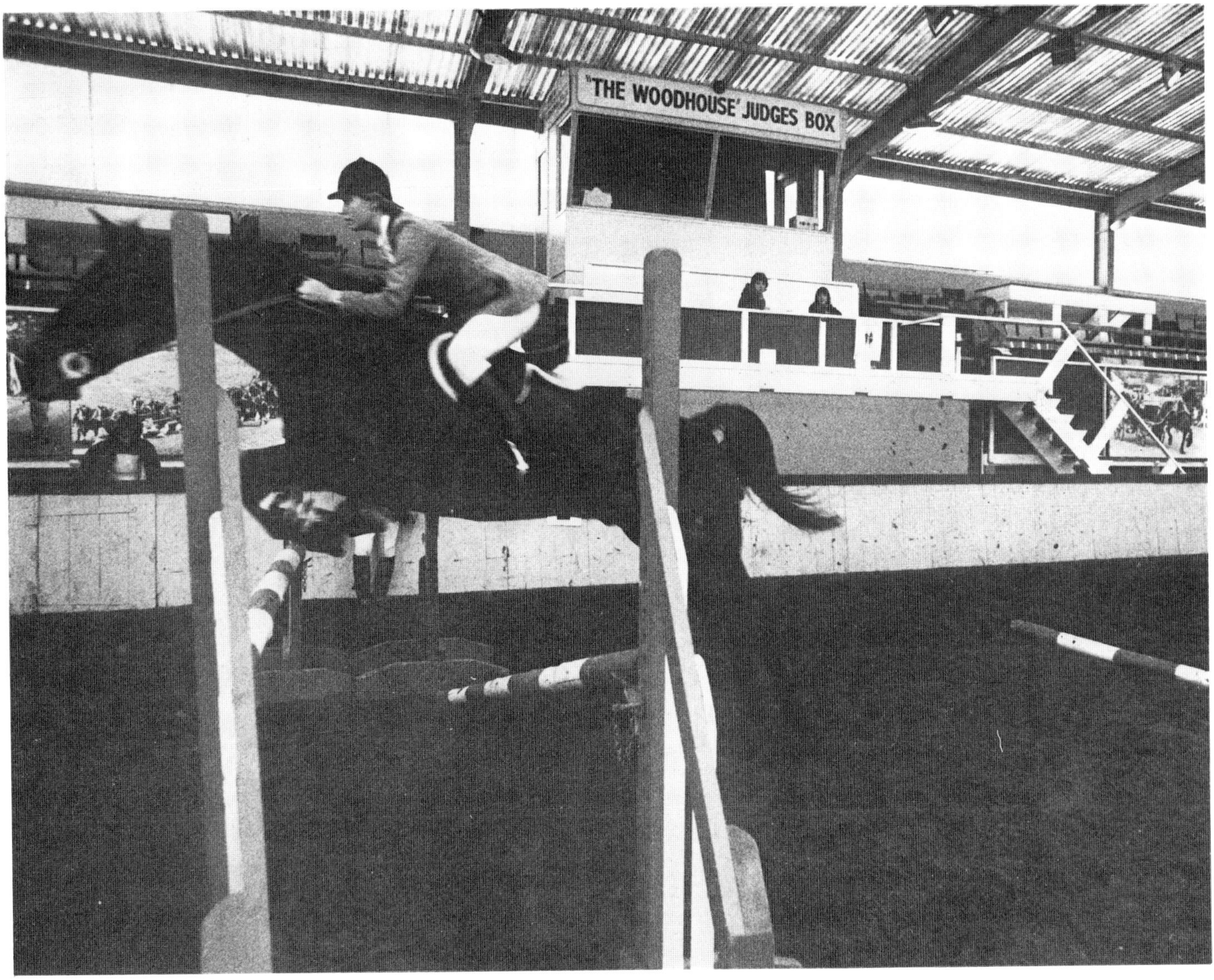
"THE WOODHOUSE' JUDGES BOX

Not all horses are easy to train, and the length of time it takes a horse to progress through each step of the training varies from horse to horse. In the first two photographs, Dick Stillwell is demonstrating how to deal with a difficult horse. By sitting on this horse, Dick is giving the rider instructions on how to turn and how the horse should hold its head. Previously, the rider was holding the reins too tightly. Dick walked the horse along the wall and, by positioning the reins correctly, he had the horse relaxed, on the bit, and every part of his body in the right position within ten minutes.

On the third day of the course, we break up into small groups. Each group must design and build its own course. We then jump the course. It's amazing how much you can learn by this exercise – showjumping courses are limited by the space of the arena, and it suddenly becomes clear to you why different obstacles are erected in certain ways! After each of us has cleared the course, Dick Stillwell tells us in no uncertain terms what we've done wrong.

On the following page you can see two different kinds of clips a horse can have. Clipping is done to help prevent the horse from sweating excessively. Usually you clip in a certain way, depending on how the horse sweats. In the photographs on the following pages you can see the horses with their various clips. The first has a chaser clip, the second has a hunter clip.

Also used to protect the horse are various kinds of rugs. In the colour section later on, the first in the picture is a sweat rug, the second a day rug, and the third a night rug.

The other two photographs on this page are of Dick Stillwell and all the pupils on the course, and of myself and Wendy Thomas leading our horses to the indoor school.

4·Horses

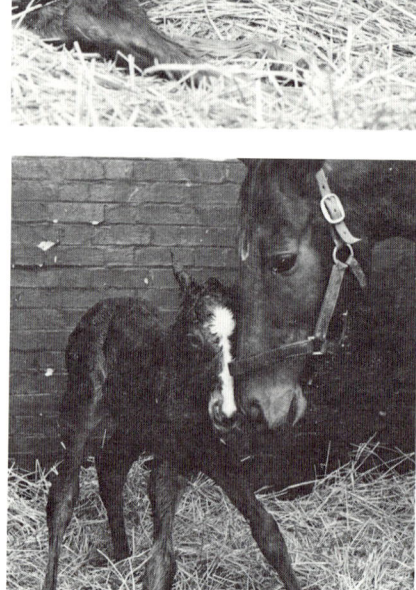

When you look closely at the horses in this chapter, you will see what beautiful creatures they are. From the first few moments of birth right through their life span, they have a frailty that is so appealing. Yet at the same time they possess such amazing strength.

It takes quite a long time before you are able to judge whether a horse has possibilities as a showjumper. Usually an expert can determine its ability when the horse is about four years old. I have to actually get on the horse and work with it for several weeks before I'm sure.

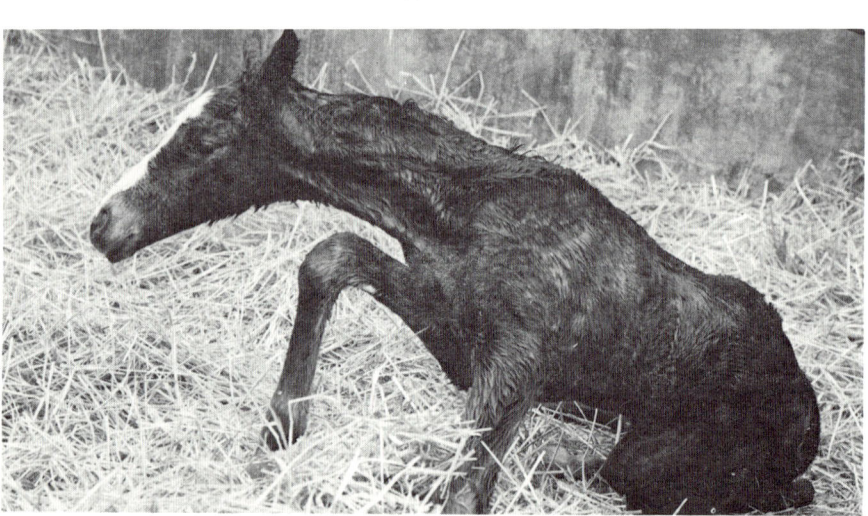

41

5·Preparing for Show

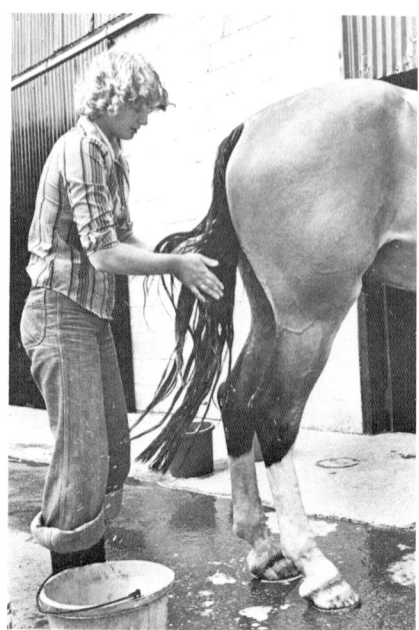

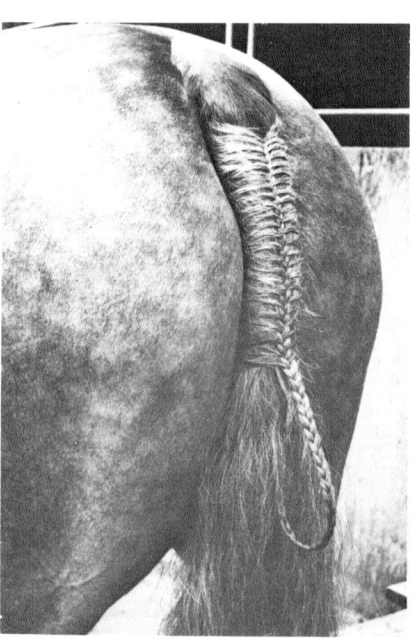

AT THE BEGINNING of the season I always find preparing for a show extremely exciting. Towards the end of the outdoor season, when we've been travelling so much and we're feeling a bit tired, the excitement isn't so great! As usual, there is a great deal of hard work involved, so we all have to be up early. First, the horses (we often take two, but sometimes there are as many as five) must be washed and groomed more carefully than usual. The same applies to cleaning the saddle and all the tack. Then the mane and sometimes the tail of the horse must be plaited – not very difficult, but it does take time. Next we load the horses into the horse box (which is Jason's favourite task, as he likes giving orders).

The photograph on the following page will give you some idea of how big our horsebox is – the horse section begins with the four little windows. We used to have a much smaller lorry and caravan, but this lorry is much better, and it is far easier for Dad to handle.

I always feel just a little reluctant as we pull away from the house. It looks so solid and comfortable, and life at the shows is always bound to be chaotic and, when it rains, distinctly uncomfortable.

You can see from the chart at the back of the book how many shows we do each year. From May to August we try and squeeze as many shows in as possible, partly in order to train and qualify the horses for Wembley, and partly to make enough money to continue on the circuit. Wembley is the goal everyone is aiming for. To do well at Wembley is everyone's dream.

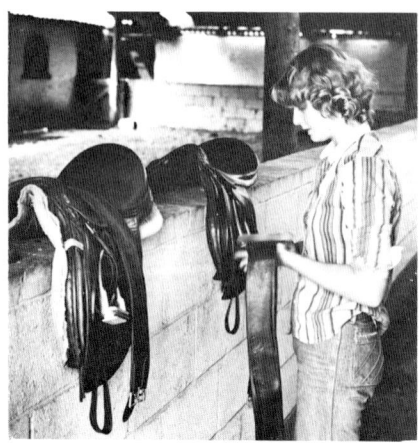

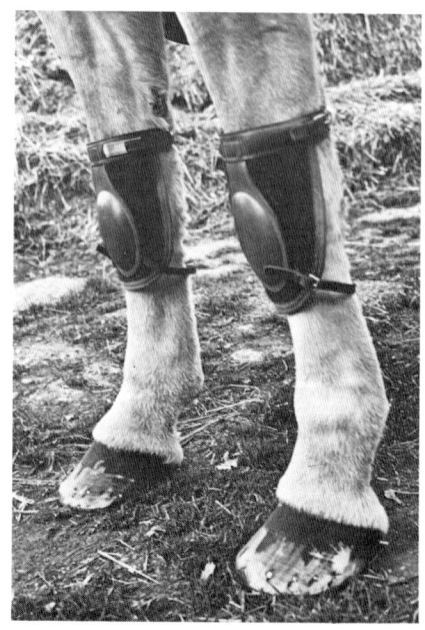

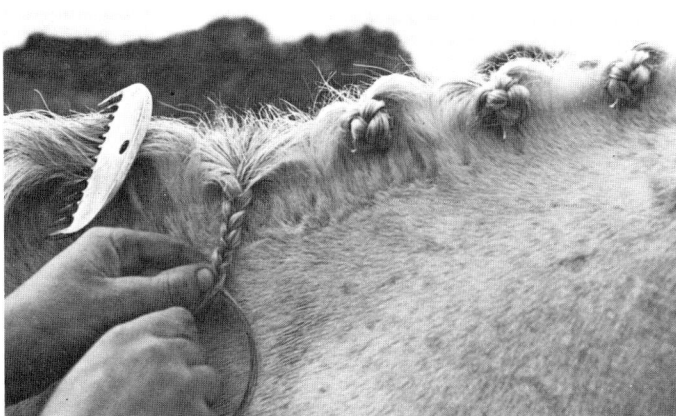

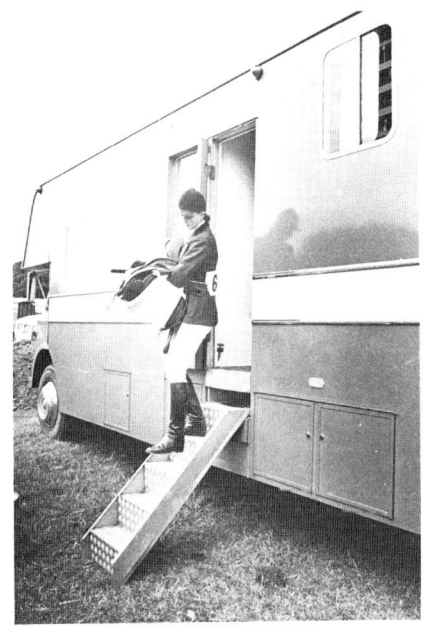

I am always very surprised when anyone asks me for my autograph. It seems a bit daft. I'm not well-known, or a star, although I suppose people do hear my name now and then, and of course one of these days I hope I will be famous!

At each show we go to there always seems to be a terrific pile of tickets, numbers and cards for each competitor. For this particular show, the Greater London Horse Show at Clapham Common, everything is highly organised. At some of the smaller shows we don't need quite so many labels and tags.

With all our equipment, clothes and horses, even our large lorry becomes quite cramped for the four of us. We try and work everything in shifts. In the opposite picture, Jill and I are getting the bridle ready in order to lead Janus down the ramp towards the ring. I then return to finish dressing myself and to get Janus's saddle.

Life is easier when the shows have their own stables for the horses. They are much easier to muck out, and give the horses more room. Even so, some of the bigger shows become like a miniature caravan city, and it takes you hours to walk to and from the arena.

Janus is quite a good horse. He simply loves to jump. He always tends to look a bit cross, as in the photograph. Once I'm on the horse, and we are on our way to the ring, I tend to lose my nervousness. Up until then, there are so many things that could go wrong, but now it is just up to us to take every jump as it comes. I'm a very calm person generally, and I think not being too emotional helps in showjumping. If your nerves are frayed and you're on edge, the horse will feel it. Sometimes when I'm in the ring I feel untidy and think my legs are going up the side of the horse, but Dad tells me they don't. I don't really know about this, but I do know that all the time we're in the ring, I'm encouraging and talking to my horse. Showjumping is very precise and demanding. Sometimes you have to jump against the clock as well as having a clear round, and you can miss by a quarter of a second or a fraction of an inch. Shouting and screaming won't put it right, so I try not to show the bitter disappointment I sometimes feel.

The last time I was really upset was when my parents sold my very favourite pony, Fates Reward. I came home three years ago from a training course, and they told me he was gone. Even though I knew I could no longer use him for showjumping, I cried for days. He was and always will be my favourite, but since I want to go into adult showjumping, this has to be done and I have now trained myself not to get too attached to any of the horses. If I hadn't done this, I'd be in a terrible state the whole time, as we are constantly changing the horses.

6·National Events

THROUGHOUT THE YEAR I try and attend as many of the national events as I can. Some of these shows include Area International Trials, and so they help me to qualify for Wembley and other big shows. These shows are by invitation only. I'm not really certain who actually decides who should be invited, but this year, because I was placed in the European Junior Championships and because I'm a member of the British Junior Team, I will probably receive an invitation to all the major shows.

Occasionally, two major events conflict. This year, for example, I didn't go to the Royal International Horse Show at Wembley at the beginning of July. I went instead to the Great Yorkshire and Peterborough Show. We decided this show was a better choice for me as there was a Calor Gas qualifier for riders under twenty-three. Winning or being placed in this event would help me get to Wembley in October.

I often compete in the Foxhunter and Elizabeth Ann classes. The Foxhunter class is for novice horses and your horse must not have won more than £75. With the Elizabeth Ann class, the competition is stiffer, but there is slightly more prize money to be won. However, for both classes you must ride a Grade C horse. My parents and I carefully plot out which events I should enter, with which horse, and the class of competition I should attempt, long before we arrive at any of the shows.

I do hate being interviewed. Here I am talking (or not talking) to BBC local radio. There really isn't very much I can say. I am always pleased to win, and I never know what my chances of winning or losing are until I've actually finished the round. I can't tell them very much about myself, except that I love showjumping.

This is a good example of two heads being better than one. Jason likes this part of the show the best – when I'm relaxing in a friend's caravan. If I've done well, the part I like best is finishing with a clear round. If I haven't done so well, escaping for a chat and a cup of tea is better.

Putting on my spurs is usually the final thing I do before going to my horse. When I was little I always used to think spurs

were so cruel, that digging sharp metal into the horse's flank would hurt him. However, used properly, a spur only gives the slightest jab into the horse's flesh. Every rider has different techniques. Some use the whip and the spurs too often for my taste. I try and treat my horses with a calm firmness. Most horses I've had respond to this, but I've had a few where we just didn't get on, and then I think it's best to sell the horse if it's mine to sell, or give it back to the owner if it isn't, because it just isn't worth all the aggravation.

Most horses go quite happily into their horse boxes or the lorry. However, every once in a while you have a stubborn horse, or one that decides to play up. The best thing you can do is talk to it quietly, and try to tease it in with a bowl of nuts, and put straw on the ramp.

A very important part of showjumping is watching the competition. You can often pick up little hints from other riders. It also helps you assess the course and prevents you from making the mistakes another rider has made. At the big shows, you can only watch if you've enough time. I usually enter two horses, but at the smaller shows, like this one, it is easier to watch the others. When I can't study things as carefully as I'd like, Mum and Dad always go and have a look and then report back.

Walking the course before jumping is extremely important as it is the only way to get a good idea of what the course is like. We must always be formally dressed with our competitor's number around our waists for this. The more experience I have with showjumping, the more I know what to look for when I walk the course, and I can work out exactly how to pace the horse for each jump. Of course, I make mistakes and then I remember Dick Stillwell's words: 'There is no such thing as a bad horse, only a bad rider.'

At this particular show we had a parade with the huntsman and the hounds. They add so much colour and excitement to the shows. With all the milling about, it sometimes seems like a festival rather than a competition.

Leafield Lad did well at this particular show. He's taking this upright jump perfectly!

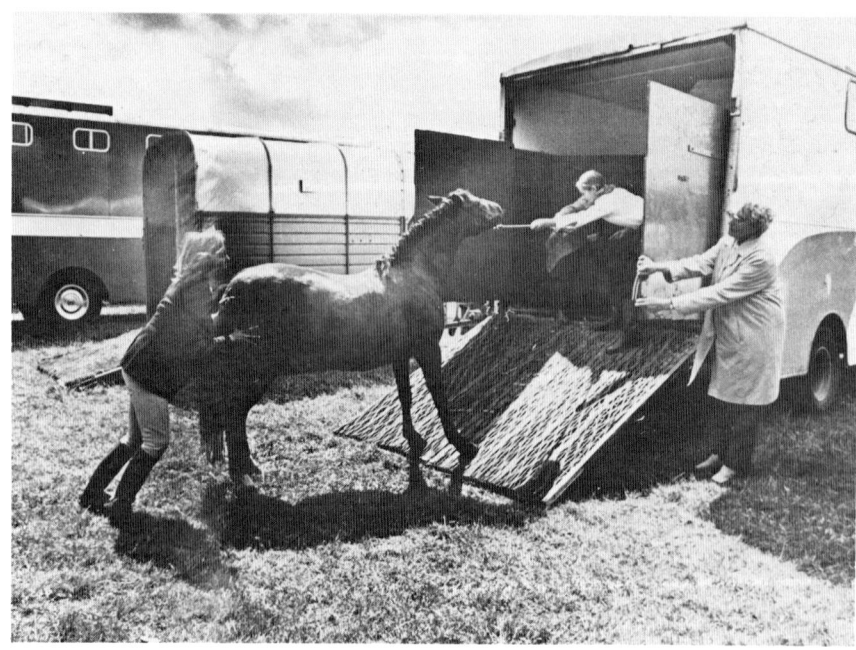

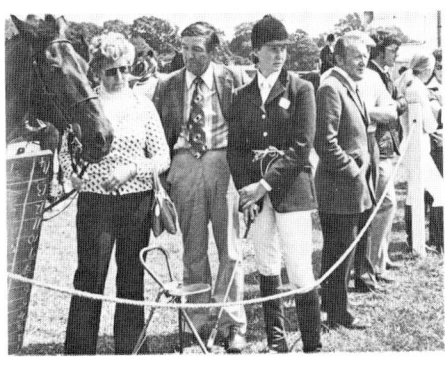

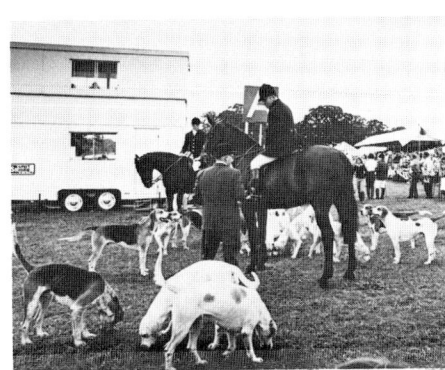

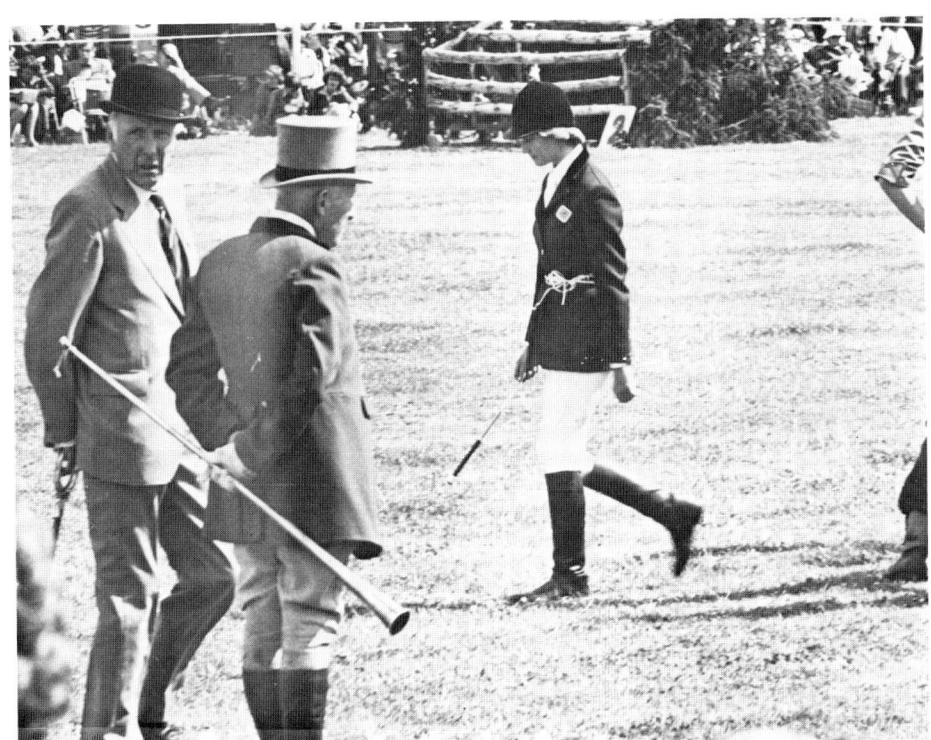

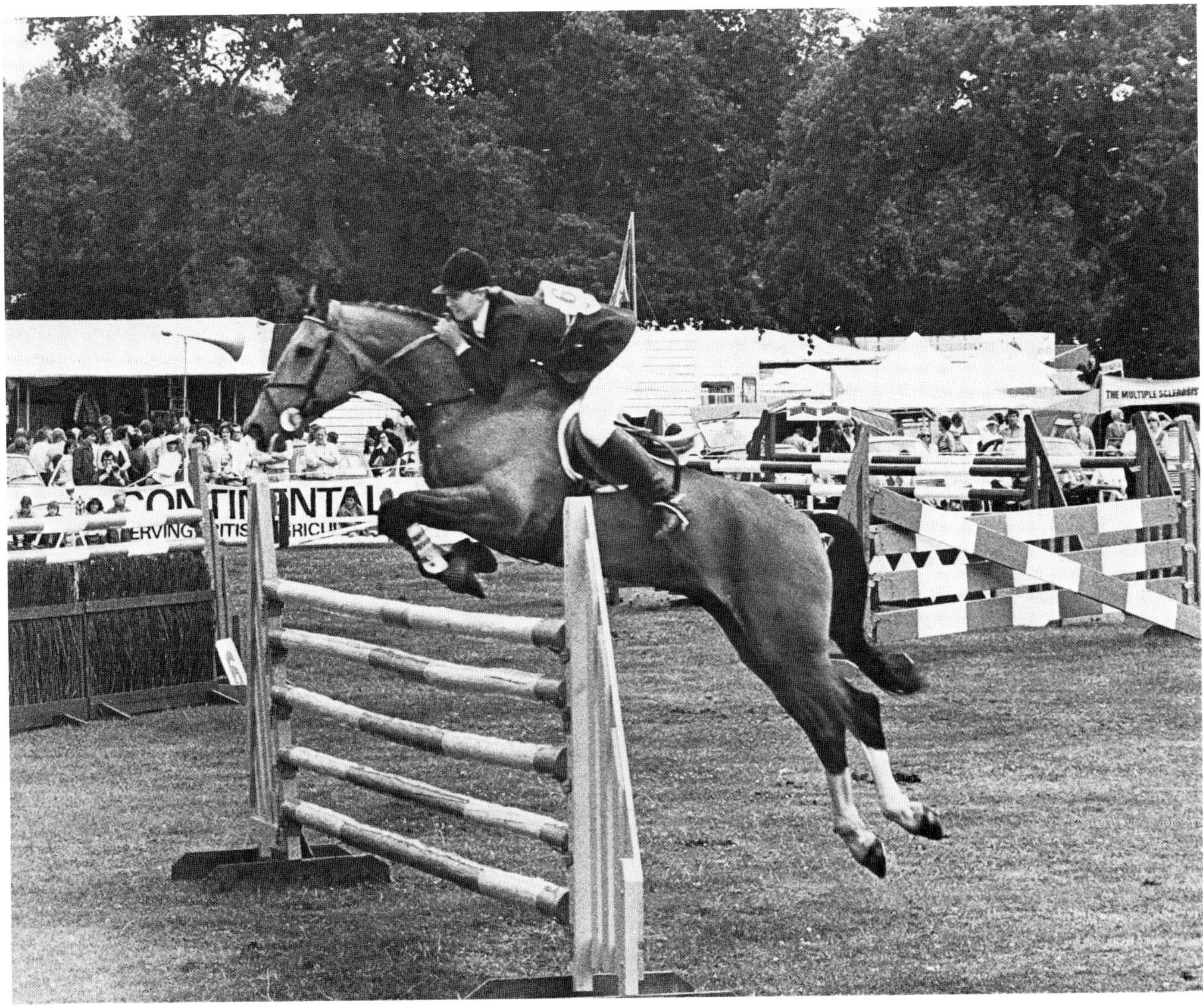
THE MULTIPLE SCLEROSIS

Several years ago, David Edgson set up Mill Lodge where now almost all showjumpers take their novice horses in the winter. At Mill Lodge we train the novice horses.

Tony Newberry and Caroline Bradley were just two of the more familiar faces present when I was there this time. Mill Lodge is especially nice as we are all more relaxed than when we are competing at the big shows. You are still assessing each other's novice horses, but you don't have to worry quite so much about your own performance.

The lovely man in the large photograph is called the Stipendiary Steward. He watches all the comings and goings of the horses. Without a set programme of events, someone is needed to make certain there isn't chaos on the course or in the collecting ring – this is the Stipendiary Steward's task, as well as making sure everyone knows the rules and sticks to them.

Mr Broughton in the first photograph is a professional horse breaker. Behind, you can see two riders practising on the outdoor course.

Mr David Edgson, the founder of Mill Lodge, is in the second photograph. The next is a shot of the farrier at work; obviously it's vital that all the horses' feet are in good condition. On a course like this we need to have all the services at hand.

The announcer calls us into the ring when it is our turn. It is not only good discipline for the horses, but it gets them used to a booming voice coming through the microphone.

On this course I took a horse we are seriously thinking of taking on – Thineas. He did very well, but we haven't made up our minds just yet.

I love the large photograph Mayotte took of the horses facing the caravans. It looks as though either the lorries or the horses are going to break into conversation at any moment!

7·International Events

THIS YEAR THE JUNIOR EUROPEAN CHAMPIONSHIP was held in Morpeth. The British team did exceptionally well, winning over the competing European teams. And I came very near to winning the individual award – I was beaten by the clock by a mere half-second, so it was a highly successful show as far as I was concerned.

Usually the Junior European Championship is held in whatever country wins the team event. However, as this is the second time we've won in succession, I think it will probably be held in another country next year – probably Spain. The show costs the host country a great deal of money, and if one team keeps winning, it does make sense that the burden should be shared by other competing countries.

When we travel to events in Europe, we always have to take massive amounts of identifying documents and papers. Sometimes we can have a smooth journey and all the border guards let us sail through. At other times, it takes hours and the guards check and double check, or else deal with all the other cars first before they attend to us. This always seems to happen when we've had a particularly bad trip, or when it is exceptionally hot!

When it pours with rain, jumping can become pretty uncomfortable, not to mention what it does to the course. Still, it is better than very hot weather, because you can never take off your jacket, and you worry about the strain the horse is under in the heat.

Leafield Lad seems to like the rain more than my other horses, and he trotted out smartly from the stables.

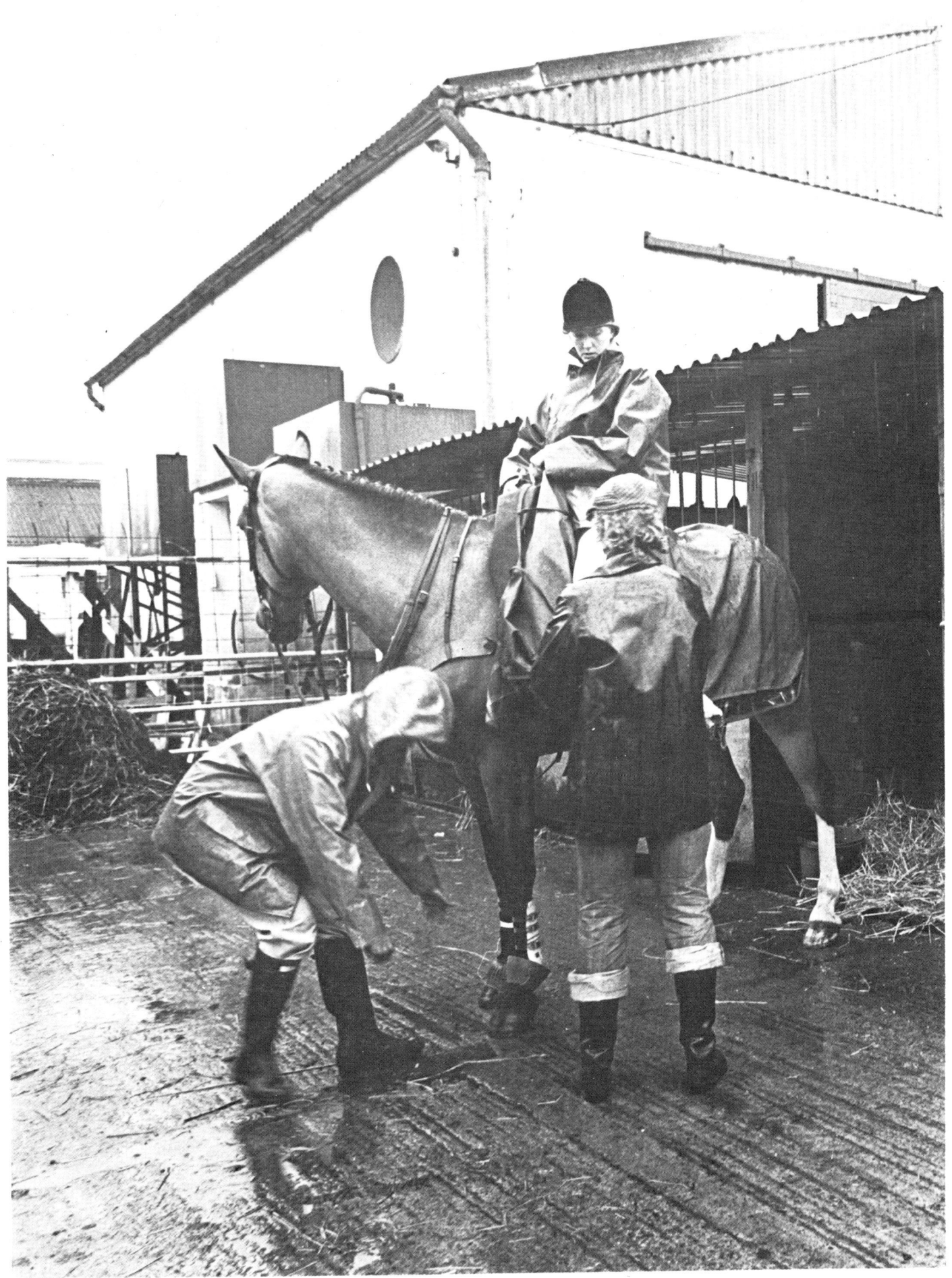

You always have to check the course very carefully, especially when it's wet, because wet conditions can alter the ground considerably and make a difference to the horse's chances. Here I'm walking it with Michael Whitaker, one of my team-mates. Sometimes it is better to go round with someone as he may see things you have overlooked.

Lionel Collard-Bovy of Belgium won the individual gold medal. I lost by half a second, and although I was pleased with my performance, I was disappointed not to have come first. I think this picture speaks for itself – there is a difference between winning and coming second.

Jill was feeling as choked as I was about coming so near to winning. There was no doubt about how well Leafield Lad and I had performed. I could only hope at that point that this would be a good omen for the future. Next time we would be that bit quicker.

After Lionel and I and Jill Kelly, who came third, had received our medals, the rest of the British and Belgian teams lined up behind us.

You can see from this photograph that almost all the horses are around the same height. For showjumping it is best to have a horse that is between sixteen and seventeen hands high. There are a number of exceptions to this 'rule-of-thumb', but since I stopped jumping ponies, I only feel comfortable on a horse of this size.

A rainy day can produce problems not only for the horses and riders, but also for the film crew. If you look closely, you will see the television cameraman is trying to dry his camera with a hair dryer! A very ingenious solution, but it didn't work, the day was just too wet and they had to give up and go home.

Television has done a great deal of good for showjumping. Before they started televising the major shows, showjumping was followed by just a minority of people. Now thousands of people share the thrills of showjumping, and top showjumpers are household names, even though a great number of people who watch have never been near a showjumping ring.

Despite the rain, you can see from the intense concentration on the faces of these riders how closely we follow each other's performances. In the front row are Steven Smith, Michael Whitaker, Robert Smith and Veronique Daems Vastapane (from Belgium). In the back row are Pat Kaye and Mrs Harvey Smith.

Waiting to start can be completely unnerving. Here something happened and I had to wait longer than usual before the starting bell. At this point I was worrying about the mud on the course, and hoping Leafield Lad would stay calm. The spectators can distract the horse and the rider. I try to concentrate entirely on the course ahead. Because of all the training the horses have had, waiting to start usually doesn't affect them too much, but you can see from Leafield Lad's ears that he isn't all that happy.

When the medals have been presented, we return to our horses and canter them round the course in a lap of honour.

Last year I went to Belgium and came home with the first prize in the Belgian Junior Grand Prix. For me, it was one of the highlights of my showjumping career. At that time Magie was called Dark Vale, and performed beautifully throughout the competition.

Winning a European competition somehow means more than winning at home. You feel as if you are doing something for your country. I feel proud to be British, to be representing my country, and to be receiving such a prestigious award.

8·Wembley – Outside the Ring with the Personalities

WEMBLEY IS THE HIGHLIGHT of everybody's year. Everyone wants to do well there. Qualifying classes for the AITs begin in March and go right on until the end of August. To qualify for the main classes at Wembley a horse has to be Grade A and it has to win at least £1200 in a year.

The atmosphere at Wembley is always different from any of the other shows. It is rather like the end of term. Once we have finished the jumping, we all go out to celebrate. We've all worked hard for this show, and when it's finished you're either pleased or disappointed with your performances, but you're always ready to start afresh, thinking that next year you'll do even better.

The special atmosphere of Wembley is probably due to the blend of Wembley tradition and the famous showjumping personalities who attend *en masse*. A lot of the activity takes place outside the ring, or at least isn't generated by the showjumping itself. It is as if there were two Wembleys – one for the competition and showjumping, the other for the carts, pony games, heavy horses and dressage! The Life Guards with their magnificent uniforms, the Household Cavalry trumpeters and the photographers and television cameras would make you feel this was a special occasion even if you didn't know it was.

Most riders attend the pre-Wembley warm-up at Park Farm in Northwood. Here there are further qualifying rounds, and this all adds to the tension and anticipation of Wembley.

Wembley itself isn't particularly attractive, with all the buildings looking like rather shabby barns. But once you pass through the curtains into the arena, Wembley is magic.

Mayotte has captured a few of the personalities and figures either relaxing or tensely watching during the six days that comprise the Wembley show. Beginning at the top left, there is David Broome and his sister, Elizabeth Edgar. David Broome is one of Britain's most outstanding Wembley competitors, but Mrs Edgar is also an important figure in showjumping circles, as is her husband, Ted Edgar. The next two are Caroline Bradley and her groom, shown here relaxing. Then there are the Commissioners pausing for a smile over their tea. Waiting and watching intently are Harvey Smith, John Greenwood and Rowland Fernyhough.

The Whitakers are a famous showjumping family and here Mr and Mrs Donald Whitaker and John have just arrived to watch Michael in his event. Here, Tony Newberry takes a break.

David Vine of the BBC is another familiar face at Wembley. His task is to set the scene for the television viewers as well as interviewing the riders, both winners and losers, the owners and other people who make up the Wembley scene.

The practice ring outside the main arena is a good place for spotting celebrities. Wembley has very few autograph hunters, mainly due to the fact that there are very strict rules governing where the public can and can not go. We riders tend to stick to ourselves – everyone behaves very professionally, knowing that someone pointing or star-gazing could upset the rider or the horse. Here, Mark Phillips is exercising on Columbus, the Queen's horse. In the next photograph he is about to enter the collecting ring. (There are essentially three rings at Wembley: the practice ring, the collecting ring where you wait to be called, and the arena where you actually compete.) Her Royal Highness the Princess Anne is chatting with Trevor Banks, a well-known owner in the showjumping world.

Philco, David Broome's horse, seems to be doing a little dance in the next photograph!

I love all the little shops that are set up at many of the shows. They are more or less a necessity for busy riders. When the season is in full swing, which is June to September, most riders have virtually no time off. We all try and attend as many shows as possible and, with the travelling, it means that you are lucky to return home even once a week. So we often have to replace our tack and clothes by buying them at the shows.

Of course, at Wembley there tend to be more shops and more excitement than at the others. First of all, Mum felt I needed a new hacking jacket. Naturally, Bernard Wetherall had a good selection but I couldn't make up my mind. Later, Jill and I looked at tack and saddles. I don't really need anything at the moment, but new ones are so lovely. We had some free advice from Mr Vallance, one of the real characters in showjumping circles!

BUTT LANE
ALLESLEY
COVENTRY

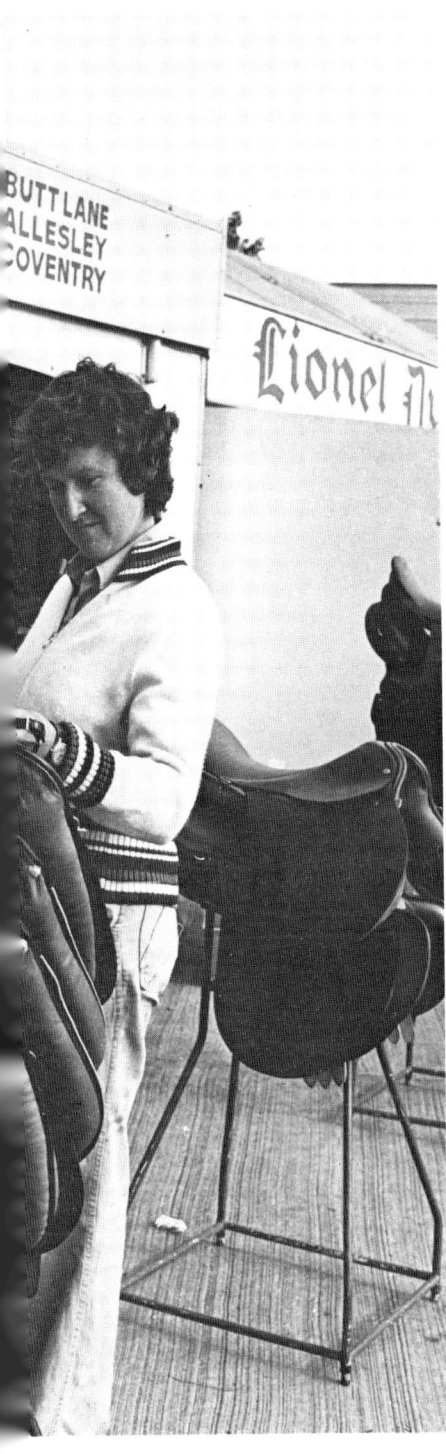

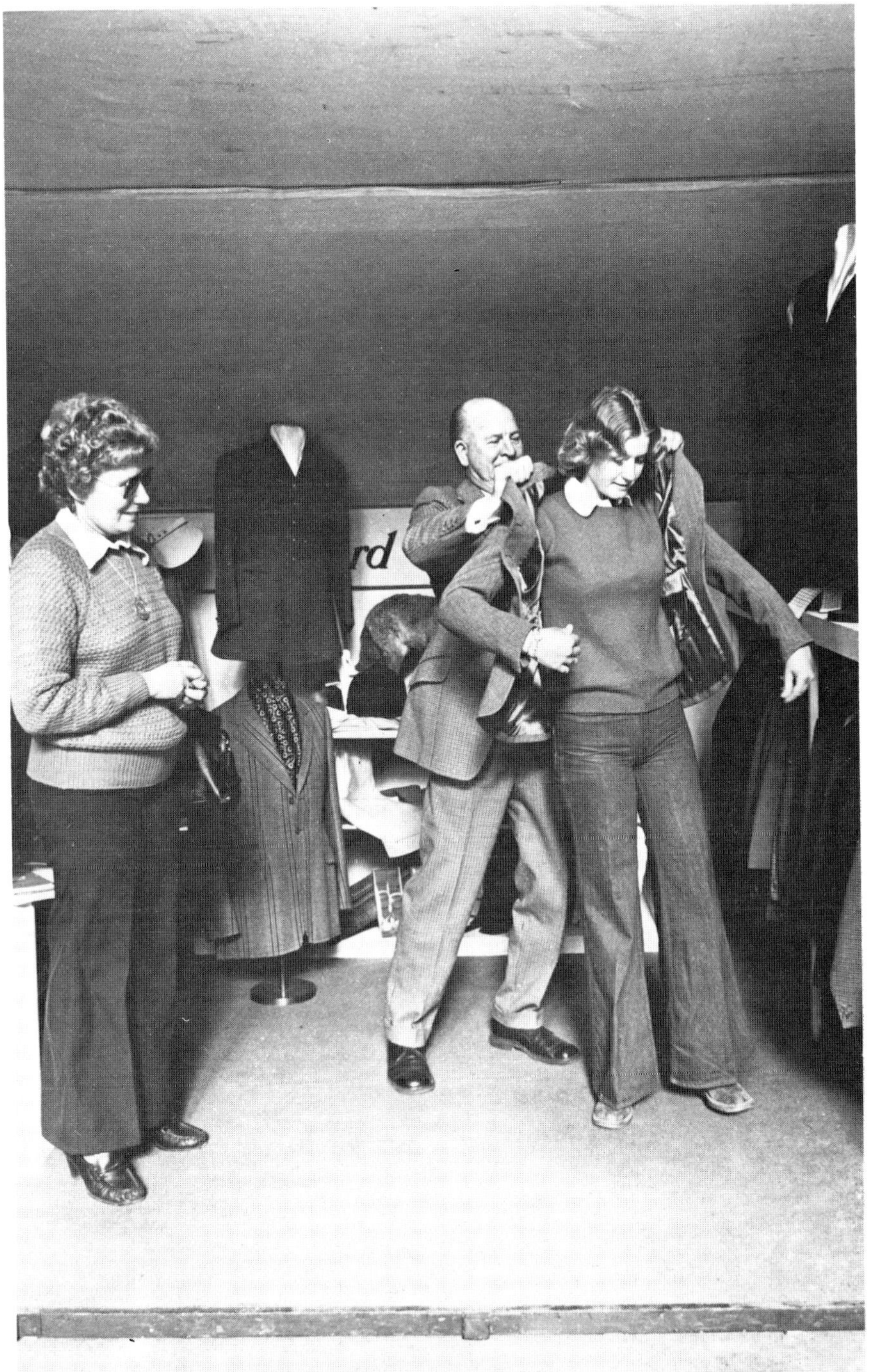

The collecting ring, just behind the arena curtain, as well as the practice ring, is another good place to see well-known faces at Wembley. First, Caroline Bradley canters around with Tigre before going on. Sally Mapleson is dismounting after what I'd say was a good round on Con Brio, judging by her expression! There Hans Winkler ponders his strategy as he waits to enter the arena. Wembley is an international event, so there are always a lot of European riders.

On the left of the heavy horses is the entrance to the arena. Very shortly they'll go through the curtain from this collecting ring to harrow the surface for the jumping. I love these heavy horses. They are beautifully proportioned and move with a special kind of grace, as their coats gleam and their harnesses glitter and shine under the brilliant Wembley lights.

James Kernan prepares to go into the ring, as Graham Fletcher and Michael Saywell walk past. If you look closely you can see the protective knee pads on James's horse, as well as the overreach boots and the brushing boots.

Graham Fletcher is now ready to leave the collecting ring on Buttervant Boy and enter the arena.

I really don't have very much time for a social life, but I do have a number of friends my age on the circuit. We usually chat about horses and jumping. We also go to the cinema together, and sometimes have parties when the shows are over. I'm often on the road on a Saturday night with my parents and Jill. The horses and the jumping always come first in this business.

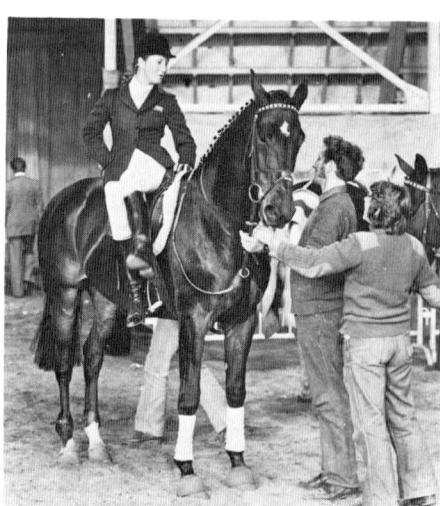

"Silver Mint"

1-20

EXHIBITORS
AND
GROOMS ONLY

FOR THIS PASS

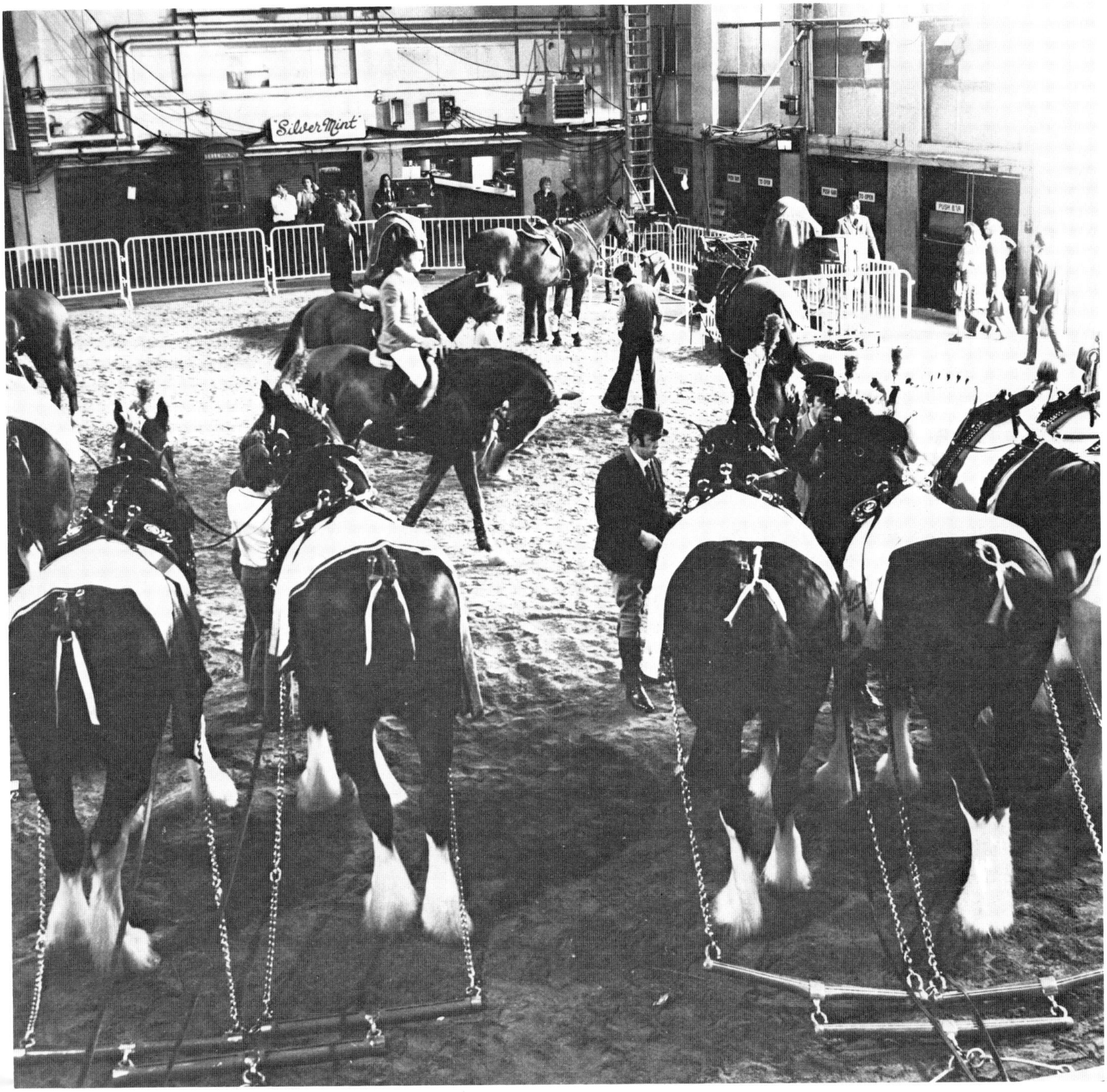

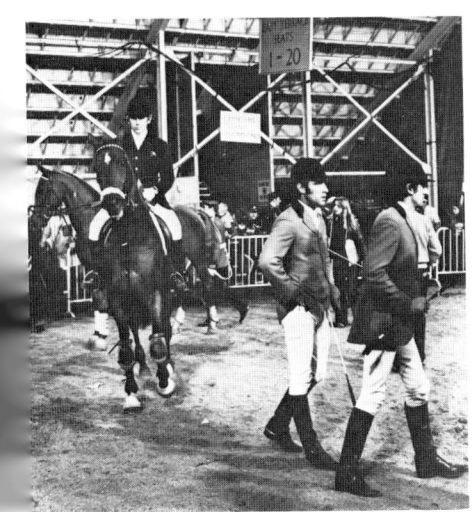

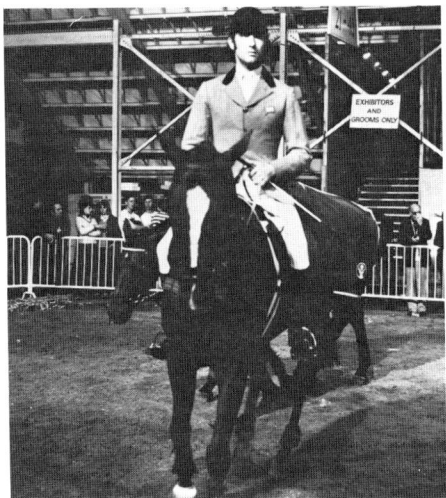

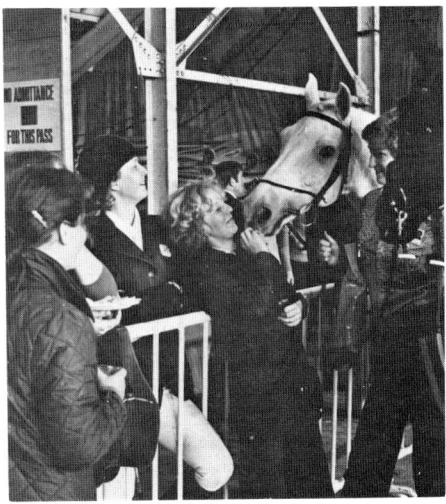

9·Wembley—Competing

For some strange reason, I've never done well at Wembley. This year was no exception. All the horses I've ever entered here, beginning with my ponies, do well right up until Wembley, and then success always seems to escape us.

The night before the classes at Wembley you have to sign a declaration form. This is to tell the judges which horse you will be jumping in each competition.

Janus and I are about to embark on the next event. Mr Appleyard is giving me encouragement, but I really just want to begin.

Janus and I execute a near-perfect jump, but our timing was a bit slow. I allowed him to make too wide a turn and we lost precious seconds.

Leafield Lad and I start off beautifully, with much tighter turns. Then, just before we pass the judges, Leafield Lad's back legs catch the top of the pole. It is something every rider dreads. Not only does it make a terrible noise, and you worry your horse may go lame, but you know you've lost, and you feel like giving up there and then. Still, for everyone's sake and for your own dignity, you must soldier on. I jump past the judges, but am relieved to disappear behind the curtain.

The puissance is one of showjumping's most exciting events for the spectator. I have yet to enter the puissance as I'm not really experienced enough, and haven't found a horse who loves jumping heights rather than spreads, which is essential for a puissance horse. In the first sequence, a rider knocks a brick out of the wall. The members of the Junior Leaders Regiment quickly replace or rebuild any part of the puissance course. They work hard, enthusiastically and with great energy, so much so that by the end of Wembley they have become favourites of the spectators and riders alike. Next is a photograph of Freddy Welch and Rossmore in their mighty winning jump over the huge wall, the final obstacle of the puissance course. As you can see, it calls for a tremendous effort from both horse and rider!

The collecting steward is another important figure at Wembley. He calls our numbers, informs us when we are due to go on, and reports any absences. I've never known anyone to miss their turn, but I suppose it could easily happen.

The dressage is quite an impressive sight. For this the competitors wear black top hats, white shirts and black jackets, and both horse and rider always look immaculate. Dressage is very precise and exacting, involving as it does the intricate leg and pace changes, which demand absolute obedience from the horse and complete concentration from the rider.

Whenever I look at the young riders on their ponies, I remember what fun I used to have. Ponies seem to take life less seriously than horses; they gallop off with the greatest zest at every opportunity. I was so proud the first time I came to Wembley with my pony.

The Junior Leaders are presented before the opening of each new section of the programme. Their bright yellow shirts and military bearing all add to the ceremony and atmosphere of Wembley.

Looking at all these photographs, I feel this is the very essence of Wembley. We are all here to jump, and if possible to jump higher and faster and more accurately than anyone else. Why do we do it? What makes us keep trying? It is very difficult to explain. For me, showjumping is my life. I can't think of doing anything else. I would like to be one of the best some day. It may sound arrogant, but given the right horse, and more experience, I hope I could do it. In showjumping, as in everything else, you really have to believe in yourself. You have to believe you're good, otherwise you'd give it all up. You can have a spate of very bad luck when nothing goes right. You have to keep thinking that tomorrow will be better, that tomorrow your luck will change. But the great thing is that you're never alone. Sometimes you may feel that you've let down your horse, and sometimes it's the other way round, but whatever the case, you're in it together and you can develop a real feeling of comradeship.

Leaving the ring when you know you haven't got a place in the top three can be a bit dispiriting. Jill and Mr Appleyard are there to console and encourage, as are my parents, but your mind keeps going back to what you should have done, and what might have been.

But only the best deserves to win. Here Freddy Welch accepts the puissance trophy from the Duchess of Kent, and Harvey Smith wins the coveted Victor Ludorum award.

Wembley finishes, but I'm off to Holland. At the end of August I went with the British Junior Team to Belgium on the CSIOJ (Concours Saut Internationale Officiale Juniors). Now I'm going on the CSI, so I'll be eligible to win prize money which you can't do when you're a junior. Then there is a Mill Lodge show to which I shall take my novice horse, and after that I've been selected to go to CSI in Switzerland and Austria. Then there is the Christmas Show at Olympia.

I'm going to keep trying, keep getting better, I hope. I've had a wonderful life so far and a lot of success for someone my age, and I'm determined to stay one jump ahead!

A SAMPLE OF JEAN'S EXPENSES

1.	Kitting and horse's equipment	£200.00
2.	Cost of horse	£500.00–£1,500.00
3.	Horse box	£2,000.00
4.	Cost of veterinary service	£5.00–£6.00 a visit
5.	Food	£10.00 a week
6.	Boots, jacket, etc for shows	£150.00
7.	Travel	£1,400.00 a year
8.	Training	£5.00 an hour

JEAN'S TYPICAL SHOWJUMPING SCHEDULE FOR A YEAR

JANUARY
Several small shows to train the novices
Mill Lodge

FEBRUARY
Hilton Park (indoor circuit, qualifier for Wembley)
Mill Lodge

MARCH
Bicton (first outdoor show of the season) AIT
– Area International Trial*
Wales and West

APRIL
Badminton AIT
Kinoulton
Doncaster (Pageant of Horses
– showing as well as jumping)
Hickstead (an international show)

MAY
Newark and Nottinghamshire
Thoresby
Windsor (an international show)
Shropshire and West Midlands AIT
North of England Equestrian Centre AIT
Hertfordshire County AIT
Burley on the Hill AIT
Suffolk AIT

JUNE
Bramham
South of England AIT
Leicester County
Three Counties AIT
Lincolnshire County AIT
Norfolk County

JULY
Buckingham
Amersham
Great Yorkshire AIT
Harringfield
East of England AIT
Adwick le Street
New Forest
Heckington

AUGUST
Hull AIT
Rutland
North of England Equestrian Centre
(Junior European Championships – Morpeth) AIT
Southport
Greater London

SEPTEMBER
Greater London AIT
Antwerp, Belgium (an international show)
Bicton
Park Farm
Mill Lodge

OCTOBER
Horse of the Year Show – Wembley (an international show)
Leeuwarden, Holland (an international show)
Mill Lodge

NOVEMBER
Montelier, Switzerland (an international show)
Vienna, Austria (an international show)

DECEMBER
Olympia (an international show)
Mill Lodge

A qualifier for Wembley